. . . So that you will remember
Where HOME is . . .

Love, Mother

Christmas, 1986

North Carolina curves gracefully to its easternmost point at Cape Hatteras, south of the famous lighthouse. At this junction warm Gulf Stream waters collide with cold Arctic waters, a perfect habitat for the many varieties of fish that thrive there. With the point perceived as the prime spot, drivers park four-wheel vehicles side by side in the sand and drop their lines expectantly over the island's edge.

A schooner on the inland waters of North Carolina breaks the steady horizon and draws the attention of everyone on shore. As it passes a day marker it illustrates freedom — freedom with guidelines. Without guides, ships from Europe discovered America's eastern shore, but not without a toll in lives and comforts. Now that passages have been explored, the love of sailing can be answered by adventurers with fewer risks.

The carved figures, jars and stemware of an antique store transist
between one home and another. Once deemed exquisite, valuable
or — at the very least — serviceable, they have become dispensable. In
Southport shops as in others across the state, they will be examined
for scars, studied for significant dates and praised once again for their
usefulness.

Grinding wheels, planers and oil cans are the unpretentious tools of
farm life. As in a barn in Wilmington, implements lie neglected for a
time, but are needed later to smooth a plank or shoe a horse.

Like nomads ascending to a lofty shrine, visitors to Jockey's Ridge State Park at Nags Head make a pilgrimage from sea level to dune peak and down again. There is shared joy in the venture and breathlessness from the climb.

A high level, four-lane bridge across the Cape Fear River in New Hanover County opened in 1969. It is equipped with a center lift that is raised and lowered like an elevator to allow passage of large ships.

Library of Congress Catalogue Number 86-82202

Hardcover ISBN: 0-917631-02-1

Photographs© 1986. Copyright 1986 in U.S.A. by Chip Henderson.

Printed in the state of North Carolina by Greensboro Printing Company, Greensboro, North Carolina.

Produced through Lightworks, Raleigh, North Carolina. 919/851-0518.

EARLY COMES THE SUN

Impressions of North Carolina's Coast

Photography by Chip Henderson

Text and Captions by Jane Collins

Design and Photographic Editing by Russell Avery, Avery Designs

Published by Capitol Broadcasting Company, Inc.

North Carolina is a startling protuberance along an already irregular coastline that takes the blows of an unrestrained sea. As if to shelter the mainland a front line of barrier islands meets the Atlantic head-on. With a shape like eastern North Carolina's it is understandable that early explorers bumped into it.

The eastern portion of North Carolina is referred to as "the coast," and that it is. Resorts and fishing villages dot its fringes, bringing seasonal patrons: surfers, "sunchildren" and charter boat fishermen. Some came generations ago and stayed. On the islands and in farming communities around the sounds and rivers they fished and cultivated the "goodliest soile."

There is disparity between the wide salt sea and narrower fresh-water alleys. Consequently, life sustained near the ocean differs from that along the rivers. On dunes sea oats wave freely; slightly denser goldenrod and broom sedge grow behind; inland, wax myrtle shrubs and live oaks thrive thickly. Gulls and terns chatter above the surf, while herons and egrets prefer fresh-water marshes.

The history of the coast, which is the story of the people and their response to a distinctive environment, bears out the dominance of the waters. Both in trade and tourism there has been, of necessity, a yielding and an adaptation to the waters' superiority. The shoreline is ever-changing but courageous and those who love the water also respect the precious acreage.

Jacketed against the cool of dawn and light-footed, perhaps for the
same reason, a fisherman heads up shore. From a myriad of good
spots in the Outer Banks, he is confident in his selection of one.

Cape Hatteras Lighthouse, built in 1869-70 with 1,200,000 Virginia-fired bricks, has for many years worn a painted pattern of alternating black-and-white spirals.

At first light or earlier a shrimp boat leaves Southport and heads out the Cape Fear River. The day will be long for the catch of fresh shrimp must be packed for shipment back at the dock.

The lights of a pier at Wrightsville Beach are reflected on the fish-rich
waters beneath and provide the effect of being widened and stretched
into shimmering patterns.

Like actors in a long-running play, the fishermen return, night after night, routinely, though happily, welcoming the rewards of each performance and not expecting them to carry over to the next curtain call.

In the coastal regions of North Carolina land and water resemble chocolate swirls in a marble cake. There is purpose though, in the variety of shapes: waters are inlets, lagoons, bays, sounds, estuaries, swamps, rivers and creeks; fingers of land are islands, peninsulas, bogs, pine savannah and maritime forests.

Chameleons, like colonists from the Old World, survive partly because they are adaptable to their surroundings. The creature that blends discreetly is now exposed by the powerful sunlight on the underside of a palmetto frond.

It can be said that day is growing, rather than breaking. From nothing — from darkness — the veil of night dissolves and the pinks form. At one time these dawns signaled the start of another farm day, but the pump is idle, the tools put up or sold and the workers called away by some other dream.

Farming has sustained the nature of man for hundreds, even thousands of years. It has evolved some — gained sophistication — but it retains the essential elements of the planter's relationship to the fruitful ground.

Not many attractions call people together. Football games do; a tragic fire or other calamity might; a political rally draws us out sometimes. But to scale a summit alongside strangers, for no other reason than to admire the created world they share: that happens rarely.

Looking like one of countless sand peaks in the Sahara, Jockey's Ridge continues to receive the sweeping, shifting and contouring of the coastal breeze. The Outer Banks are known for their dunes, but here is their highest — a 138-foot high sandpile. No other Atlantic or Gulf coast dune can compare with it.

Tryon Palace in New Bern is seasonally decorated with ivy garlands. It became both capitol building and home of Governor William Tryon, who found the colonists in a generous mood when he asked for it in 1765.

The Jones House is part of the Tryon Palace complex and the governor's eastern office. It is draped with Christmas accessories in the tradition of some of New Bern's many eighteenth-, nineteenth-, and early twentieth-century homes.

Man has always gone to sea. Whether the vessel was a bold Viking "long ship" of the eleventh century or the passenger liner *Queen Elizabeth*, the urge to sail is undeniable. Now four adventurers can sample the great Atlantic in a modern sloop and be home for supper.

Because the sea is unrelenting and not respectful of persons large or small, it is wise to make a gradual acquaintance by floating in the shallow surf. Nearly everyone, though, after adjusting to the shoving waves and pulling tide, wants to come back again and again.

Like the other lighthouses and towers along the Atlantic coast, Cape Hatteras Lighthouse is meant to be seen. For in the spotting of it, the sailor is warned. He knows to be cautious, for he is crossing what is known as the "graveyard of the Atlantic," resting place for hundreds of ships who did not escape barely-submerged sandbars known as Diamond Shoals. To minimize the risks, Cape Hatteras Lighthouse was built to be America's tallest, a distinguished 208 feet.

Another tall structure, a fire tower in eastern North Carolina, is designed to avert tragedy. Like the lighthouse, height offers the advantage. But while the lighthouse must be seen to be effective, the fire tower must provide a vantage point for finding the danger spots. A fire started by lightning or careless woodsman has the potential for great destruction, but the ability to spot it and contain it quickly may depend on the fire tower and the alertness of its sentinels.

The humble sea oat that greeted the colonists is still part of the stark, unpretentious landscape of the coast. It serves a purpose, too: the perennial native grass, flexible yet wind resistant, helps protect sand dunes from dispersion.

The silhouetted figure of proud horse and rider represents a lesser known treasure of Cape Hatteras and eastern North Carolina. Registered Spanish mustangs, or banker ponies, number fewer than thirty in the area and are descendants of horses of the sixteenth century conquistadors.

A dramatic pylon of gray granite guards the site where two curious and courageous brothers flew a heavier-than-air, four-cylinder glider 120 feet across the sand and into a new age. The Wright Brothers National Memorial, marking that 1903 spectacle, stands at the summit of Kill Devil Hill on the Outer Banks between Kitty Hawk and Nags Head.

The simplest form of entertainment can yield gratifying results, and although the baseless sand house must fall to the tide, the concept is lasting: rarely is a split-level, condo or southwestern adobe constructed but a castle.

Only courage and awesome determination drove Americans' ancestors to flee England and risk the perilous Atlantic to try to settle the wilds of a new continent. When one steps onto the *Elizabeth II* on the Manteo waterfront, imagines that this is the whole of his world for numberless months and that if he sees shore again his safety is still uncertain, he is surely somewhat awed. The full-size replica of sixteenth century sailing ships is complete with kegs, bottles and cooking utensils typical of those significant voyages.

The first waters explored by the *Elizabeth II* were those of the Pamlico Sound and Neuse River when a grant from Capitol Broadcasting Company brought the ship to Beaufort and New Bern and 15,000 delighted visitors.

Some twenty acres of azaleas, camellias, live oaks and cypress trees
make up the gardens at Orton Plantation. Overlooking Cape Fear
River, these grounds, along with the grand southern antebellum Orton
home, were formerly a rice plantation of the early eighteenth century.

Vertical fence slats, in softly curved, random pattern help accentuate the contrasting features of shorelines and, in addition, support the occasional grass patches in sheltering the dunes against the winds.

People in landlocked communities may have other compensations, but those living near water wonder what they could be. A lakeside dock and boat, available at a whim, make simple but incomparable recreation.

Carefully prepared soil and healthy seeds bring a crop fit for the farmer's table and his marketing outlets. Add the favorable climate and plenteous water sources in eastern North Carolina and youthful sprouts will become tender vegetables welcomed across the state.

With a tug of triumph two fishermen haul their bounty ashore. They have proven again that Cape Hatteras Point is one of the best — if not *the best* — fishing spots on all of the Outer Banks. Their craft and their nets are merely functional, not expensive, frilly or state-of-the-art, but the pleasure they help provide is untarnishable.

Bearing its cargo, a freighter traverses the waters of a North Carolina sound, one of the last of the links in the chain of commerce.

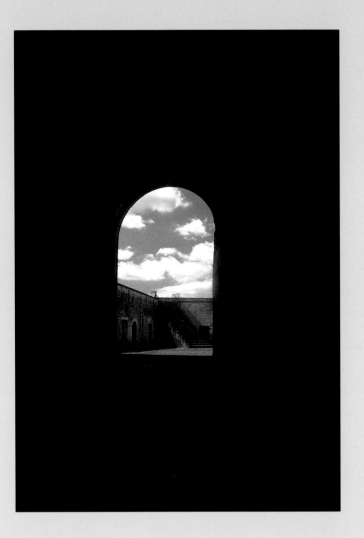

On the eastern end of Bogue Banks, Fort Macon, now a state park, brings to mind the fierce fighting of the Civil War and earlier, the threat of searaiders to Beaufort Inlet.

Along an isolated stretch of Bald Head beach are several quaint houses. They were originally provided by the government for the keepers of Cape Fear Lighthouse and their families until 1958 when the lighthouse was deactivated.

It's a placid dockside scene that one finds often enough today, but Beaufort, third oldest town in the state, was a vulnerable port city. Beaufort experienced pirate raids by the Spanish in the 1740's, harassing by the British at the close of the American Revolution, and was claimed by first the South and then the North during the American Civil War. In this century, it is known for fine fishing and a large collection of very old homes.

A favored chunk of North Carolina real estate is Atlantic Beach. Year after year families come to swim, wade, float, and dig in the sand. Houses along the shore suggest that it is not the square footage of personal property that counts, but rather the width of the clean beach and the expanse of the great ocean.

North Carolina has its share of golf enthusiasts, some of whom are drawn to the challenging fairways on Bald Head Island. Still lovely with its lagoons and palm tree clusters, the course was a marshland and forest only a few years ago.

Of the rich green of his family farmland, a twentieth-century planter might agree with the words of David the Psalmist, "The lines have fallen to me in pleasant places; indeed, my heritage is beautiful to me."

As if it cannot stay out of sight any longer, the sun's rays push out of a cloudy box and dazzle a rippled surf at Atlantic Beach.

For nearly a century, "Old Baldy" served as sentry on Bald Head Island, its light guiding vessels across Cape Fear Bay and into the river channel. Octagon-shaped and sturdy, the lighthouse is North Carolina's oldest.

The Anglican church was established in Edenton when the town
was incorporated in 1722; St. Paul's Church building was built about
fifteen years later. The churchyard, therefore, is even older than the
very old church building. In colonial times the church provided burial
for citizens of the town as well as for members. These graves bear the
remains of individuals significant in North Carolina history, such as
colonial governor Charles Eden, after whom the town was named.

A curtain is falling on the sun's finale. All day it has performed with starlike consistency, but now in the remarkable final hour, the sun has center stage.

Some of the most fished waters of the Outer Banks are in and around Oregon Inlet. The inlet did not exist during colonial times, but opened during a hurricane in 1846, and is considered crucial to the fishing industry that is centered in Wanchese on Roanoke Island.

"When you do dance, I wish you a wave o' the sea, that you might ever . . ." dance.
Shakespeare said it, but it is worth repeating; in another age and on another shore
the dance goes on.

Two perspectives of Ocracoke reveal some of its pristine charm. A weathered shed on the dock protects fishing equipment; Silver Lake dips in from Pamlico Sound; the lighthouse stands over low houses. Ocracoke was settled in the seventeenth century; its early history is colored with tales of Blackbeard the Pirate who was killed nearby in 1718.

Although the faithful sentinel is in retirement, "Old Baldy" continues to enhance the shoreline and complement a cloud-etched sunset.

The sun, generous with color to the end of day, strikes the lagging tide with phosphorescent splendor.

A child is never completely owned, nor *known*, by anyone, for her thoughts belong to her alone. The adult world can best contribute to those thoughts by emphasizing the desirable truths it has learned and by cushioning the impact of less beautiful realities. The Day School at St. James Episcopal Church in Wilmington, like many other learning centers, has such a mission.

The first distinguished resident of 400 Front Street in Wilmington was Governor Edward Bishop Dudley. In 1836, he became North Carolina's first governor to be elected by popular vote. In the Georgian-style mansion, Governor Dudley, who was also president of a railroad, helped plan a rail line that was at the time, the world's longest. Years later, the so-called Governor Dudley Mansion was owned by James Sprunt, cotton merchant, philanthropist, British vice consul and author of *Chronicles of the Cape Fear River,* 1914.

The oldest church building in North Carolina is found in Bath, North Carolina's first incorporated town. St. Thomas Episcopal Church, formed in 1701, also is recognized as one of only three colonial brick churches remaining in the state. George Whitefield, renowned English evangelist and contemporary of John and Charles Wesley, preached there in 1739.

The Reverend A.C.D. Noe, Rector Emeritus, who came to St. Thomas in 1936 and retired in 1953, is remembered for his efforts to restore the ancient church. He died in 1978 and was buried there, outside of the window, having seen the building renewed and honored for its part in the state's rich heritage.

On the sound behind Wrightsville Beach, two dissimilar boats illustrate a fairly obvious fact: boats are not alike because people are not alike and are not drawn to the water for exactly the same purposes. Even among fishermen, the catch for one is not the envy of all others: the seas hold a variety of bounty.

At rest now, surrounded by still water and the sun's last burst of color, a shrimp boat in Southport is only temporarily alone. The boat was built for working, not for luxury, and like a drone bee, work it will. An unharvested bed of shrimp brings no income.

With synchronized rowing, men representing sailors of Sir Walter Raleigh's era exhibit the *Silver Chalice*, the *Elizabeth II*'s companion vessel known as a "ship's boat." Smaller boats, carried on decks of mother ships, were used to ferry men and supplies onto land when waters were shallow.

A ferry of the 1980's travels between Hatteras and Ocracoke islands with its cargo of vehicles and passengers. The jaunt takes about forty minutes and offers motorists an opportunity to savor the breeze as one shoreline recedes and another emerges.

Get a running start, push the control bar out, lift your legs and, hopefully, you and your forty-pound rogallo wing are aloft over Nags Head and Jockey's Ridge State Park. Fledgling glider riders succeed here, partly because the dune is high, but not mountainous. One-, two-, and six-day lessons are offered by a first-rate hang-gliding school.

Much further south, below Cape Hatteras, islands of the Outer Banks begin to draw closer to the mainland. Collectively called Cape Lookout National Seashore, the park contains about 16,000 acres and is made up of Portsmouth Island, Core Banks and Cape Lookout, and Shackleford Banks. Like banks to the north, Core Banks is eroding on its oceanfront and little can be done to prevent it. However, a process of nature that results in an overwash of the low sand dunes is helping to retain the original, though diminishing shape.

In the early morning, distinctive shapes of stained-glass and came cast muted patterns of softly colored light near the brick-tiled chancel floor. In Edenton, the building of St. Paul's Episcopal Church is second oldest of the state's churches and its parish was organized and chartered before any other in North Carolina.

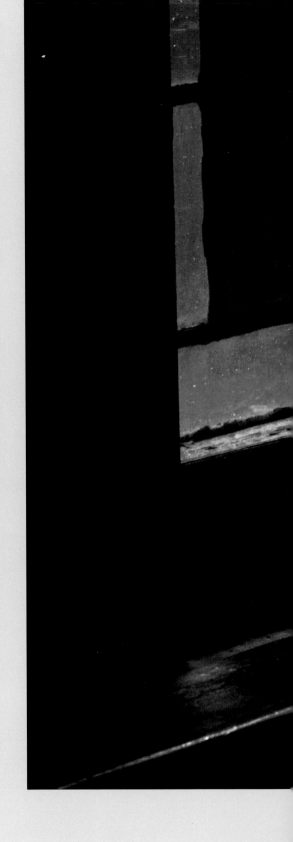

Add a candle and glass chimney and the light of early days reflects on a window of Ann Street Methodist Church, perhaps as it did when the building served as a Union army hospital during the American Civil War. One of the windows honors Robert and Mary Chadwick, former members who befriended a Chinese stowaway named Charlie Soong. Soong, who later returned to China as a missionary, married and fathered three famous daughters. One of them married Chinese Nationalist leader Chiang Kai-shek, apparently after having influenced him in his conversion to Christianity.

The challenge of catching a bluefish is exhilarating for a time, but the exchanges between the fisherman and his companion — spoken informally amid phrases of support and encouragement — may have lifelong benefits.

In the marshes of coastal North Carolina, a tree, survivor of many winds, illustrates a natural phenomenon that generally fits human character, too. The tree has been bent and strengthened by exterior forces, but the effect is esthetically pleasing, and growth and good health are established.

In the village of Rodanthe, on Hatteras Island, the old Chicamacomico Lifesaving Station, one of seven once operative, is now a proud historic site. The main building, together with the lookout tower and other structures, is the most complete surviving station on the North Carolina coast. It attests to the valiant lifesaving efforts of brave men.

Ocracoke Lighthouse, the oldest beacon still operating on the coast of North Carolina, is unique in its rural setting. Instead of sandy isolation, the conical pillar of whitewashed masonry stands inside Ocracoke Island's only community.

"The Showboat" of World War II, better known now by her military
designation, the U.S.S. North Carolina, is a battleship permanently
moored in Wilmington. Annually, more than 200,000 tourists visit
this national historic landmark, inspecting its compartments, eight
decks and museum.

Perhaps the simplest and most authentic vessel of America is the canoe. Two paddlers propel their craft, not along a mountain stream, but in Wilmington, on Greenfield Lake.

A theatrical technique which writer Paul Green called "a symphonic drama," is the vehicle for portrayal of his play, "The Lost Colony," performed each summer in Manteo. Drawing from early accounts, his script is an authentic representation of the people and times and does not offer an unprovable solution to the mystery, but stirs and entertains audiences at a waterfront amphitheatre.

Patches of sunlight fall in narrow rows among fresh-water grasses. Above the waterline they send forth oxygen; below it they become food for aquatic organisms.

A favorite portion of the pier is familiar
to a veteran fisherman, as recognizable
to him as a shady fishing hole on a lake.

Silently with scarcely anyone to notice, the
reliable sun emerges to uncover the colors
that were blanketed with its disappearance.
A long dock parallels the shoreline on the
sound behind Jockey's Ridge, the evergreen
shrubs and larger trees contributing to
the ecology of the area.

Along Cape Hatteras National Seashore fishermen like to meet their prey halfway. When they drive to the edge of the water and plant their poles close to the comfort of their jeep, they have combined convenience with pleasure.

They don't always strike above water, but fish are abundant in lakes, rivers and sounds throughout eastern North Carolina. Bass, perch and sunfish are some of the bait-hungry varieties that sustain the region's reputation for great fishing.

From the northern shore of Roanoke Island, one looks toward Albemarle Sound. Some of America's earliest settlements were informally established along the Albemarle shores and in time villages grew into thriving colonial towns.

Ever winding, changing course, then detouring yet again, the salt marshes and tidal creeks of the Carolina coastlands seem particularly mysterious and alluring at the edge of day.

Having navigated the narrow alleys, a homebound boater follows a wider course. With the day quickly disappearing, he will probably leave his particular pursuits for tomorrow.

Boats of assorted sizes berth at a Wrightsville Beach marina; some are permanent homes for their owners. Wrightsville is one of North Carolina's oldest resorts and spreads across an entire island.

Airlie Loop Road, an inviting bit of highway, leads to Airlie Gardens near Wrightsville Beach. The gardens are part of an old plantation where live oaks and brilliant azaleas encircle a serene lake with its storybook swans.

Hazardously shallow and thick with cypress trees, Lake Mattamuskeet in Hyde County greets the day much as it did in 1715 when Machapunga Indians lived on the eastern edge. Largest of the Carolina bay lakes, Mattamuskeet, "the moving swamp," is winter residence for 100,000 ducks and geese, along with one-fifth of North America's whistling swans and some bald eagles.

Crab pots marked by buoys have been dropped over the side of the boat and retrieved many times. Who could count the bounty or set the scales for a lifetime of effort? One muses at the rowboat's name: *Full Circle*. Perhaps if it were freshly painted, the boat would be at a stage of completion. Instead it possesses the quality of enduring. Someone should always be casting nets from it and telling fish stories.

People adapt to the sea, not the other way around. Through inspiration, trial and improvement, wind boards came into being and spread from the west coast to the east. After only two decades of existence the sport of windsurfing has been added to Olympic competition.

The palmetto green of Bald Head Island pervades much of the subtropical wilderness. Careful development of parts of the island maintained a suitable environment for herons and ibises. Loggerhead turtles lay eggs in large numbers.

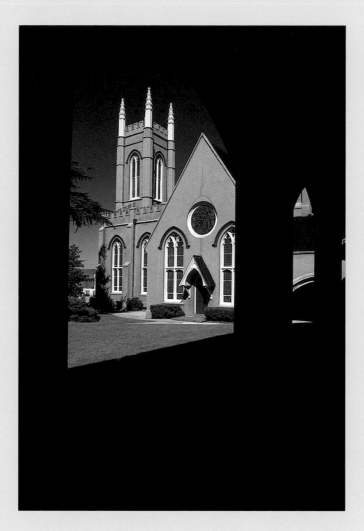

At Third and Market Streets in Wilmington, framed in the arch of a cloister, stands St. James Episcopal Church, oldest church in the Cape Fear district. The parish was created in 1728; the original building was erected between 1751 and 1770. The present structure, built about 1839, is a conspicuous monument denoting belief in God as inspired by early worshippers.

Modern sail and motor boats, maneuverable and available, replace craft designed in the Outer Banks centuries ago. A goal of designers is to combine beauty and function. Maybe they feel that the beauty and productivity of the sea deserve it.

Sometimes there is suffering: too much rain or too little. The winds ravage and then back down. Eastern waterlands, so close to benevolent nature, are also vulnerable to its occasional rudeness.

His attention belonging for the moment to someone or something that can only be imagined, a barefooted, Tar Heeled little boy appears to adapt to a shell-dotted beach. His heritage is the clean, peaceable sands about him. He knows nothing of the first explorations here, only of his own discoveries. The planting and plowing, the wars that touched these coastlands, the changing shorelines are not yet among his concerns. His joy and wonderment are in the present.